MORE
Poetic Views
of
Life

Laurie Wilkinson

This edition published in Great Britain in 2014 by

MyVoice Publishing
33-34 Mountney Bridge Business Park
Westham
PEVENSEY
BN24 5NJ

ISBN 978-1-909359-44-4

Cover Photo: The author with a termite nest.
Photo by the author.

Introduction

About this time last year (November 2013), the idea that I would have a book of my poetry published was not even a consideration. That I had my first book published in April 2014 was an excellent surprise, even more so that it has done so well, with poems from it published in both national and local newspapers.

Thus it is extremely difficult to describe my elation that my second book with 60 new poems, is actually in front of you now.

I have not changed my style of writing poetry but hopefully I have learnt and improved over the last year to provide a better book of poems for any reader. Again the poems cover a wide spectrum of themes based on my observations, opinions and outlook of life. Please enjoy my second book of poetry.

Laurie Wilkinson Bsc (hons) RMN

Acknowledgements

As with my first book I would like to thank my wife Iris, for her patience and support along with many friends and family for their encouragement. My thanks also to Anderida Writers group in Eastbourne for their continued support and advice, with a special mention to two dear friends, Shona in New Zealand and Diana M for their honest and helpful feedback after initially reading my poems for me.

I also appreciate all who bought my first book, especially The 42nd Highland Regiment of foot (1815), Napoleonic Society who generously supported me. Also thanks to The Sussex Newspaper Group for their publicity articles, poem publishing and video which gave me an increased impetus and motivation for this second book.

I would again like to express my thanks to My Voice Publishing for their guidance, support and advice with this publication.

Lastly and by no means least, thanks to the reader for your interest and again even more to anyone buying this book who will ensure that like my first book, a donation from sales will go to the excellent charity Help for Heroes.

Contents

Laurie Wilkinson

ROMANCE

Laurie Wilkinson

A Wildest Dream

Looking back inside ourselves
How wistfully we can recall,
Times and places that have gone,
Wildest dreams that had to fall.

Many an act or adventure bold
That mostly could not be,
Something that was not known,
Or meant for you and me.

Eyes and ears that are seeking
Sights and sounds passing by,
Driven by some unknown force
That came from sea or sky.

So I listened to all the melodies
And then had to pick a card,
Knowing surely it would lose
And thus be forever marred,
By decisions that are Hobson's
Though seen to be our choice,
But it's very hard to call out
If the music has your voice!

Looking back inside ourselves
How wistfully we can recall,
Times and places that have gone,
Wildest dreams that had to fall.

I can still remember days
And wonder what we think,
Of those once upon a times,
When life was on the brink.
Music, love and laughter
That took stars from on high,
To put down for us to see
What light just had to die.

--ooOoo--

Laurie Wilkinson

Eye Line Smile

It doesn't take much to lift a heart
Or cause our soul to swoon.
Just loving words or chaste kiss,
Can lift us round the moon.

Whether eyes are dark or light
They can twinkle and bewitch,
Causing a thrill right through you
As if someone clicked a switch.

Seeing can makes hearts flutter
With pulses racing with a touch.
There is no magic spell for this,
Just that we love so very much.

Contented sighs descend on us
Like some heaven sent cascade.
And nothing will keep us apart,
Even rivers, hill or barricade!

A plain face may cause sunrise
When it breaks into a smile,
And when that beam is loving
Joy will fast flow like the Nile!

Whether eyes are dark or light
They can twinkle and bewitch,
And if they sparkle just for you
Your whole life will enrich.
For in a world that's tough at times
Where you strive hard for reward,
Being drawn to loving eyes
May bring ecstatic life accord!

--ooOoo--

A personal poem for you, or for...

...your family, events, birthdays, anniversaries or business. Give me the details for your poem and leave the rest to me!

Published works so far:

Poetic Views of Life - £4.99
More Poetic Views of Life - £4.99
Reviews of Life in Verse - £4.99
Life Scene in Verse - £6.99
Life Presented in Verse - £6.99
Poet Reveals All - £9.99

"An inspirational, witty and wise read."

TED & BETH
of Laurie the Poet

Our poems are in all of his books
(6 currently); please read about us -
f: Ted n Beth of Laurie the Poet

Every sale ensures a donation to
'Help for Heroes'

The Psychy Poet

Contact us on: t: 07967 355236   e: lw1800@hotmail.co.uk
w: www.psychypoet.com   f: The Psychy Poet Laurie Wilkinson

Laurie Wilkinson

Call of Nature

Her touch gave him an electric shock
Down to his very heartbeat station,
And fixed a smile upon his face
Like a state of besotted inebriation.

For the feelings of love and lust
Are not so very far apart,
And while an outer sensation
It will be felt more in the heart.

So no amount of lateral thinking
Will save him from his fate,
If a pretty face and hands work,
Their magic, it's too late.
To separate rhyme or reason
So many a big man will fall,
At the first hurdle of his senses
As though he'd hit a wall!

For the feelings of love and lust
Are not so very far apart,
And while an outer sensation
It will be felt more in the heart.

Such is the power of natures wish
To spellbind those too ripe,
From allowing a chosen journey
So they must conform to type.

And surrender any last protest
They must then heed the call,
For to act on their hearts wishes
Is better than not to hear at all.

--ooOoo--

Rock Star

At times life seems a struggle
You just don't know what to do,
But you will always find a way
When someone really loves you.

They will help to pick you up
And send you back on your way,
So even if you stumble more
You will feel their love each day.

The best way to deal with strife
Is to take the worry and share,
As any help and encouragement
Will remind you that they care.

A simple man can be like a king
And lifted on towards his glory.
Knowing that he has an ally who,
Will support and tell his story.

This ally will help to pick you up
And send you back on your way,
So even if you stumble more
You will feel their love each day.

When you've won and are the star
And all the accolades you pack,
You will look round for your "rock"
But they've gone three paces back.
Thus leaving the spotlight all on you
As by the admirer's you are trailed,
You will know deep in your heart
Without your rock you'd have failed!

--ooOoo--

Laurie Wilkinson

Arrival of Love

When love arrives the first time
You will never be quite the same,
Despite wise words of people older
Your heart is hobbled, you are lame.

For you will think you know it all
With the fluttering thrill of love,
Turning grey into a blinding light
As if sent down by heaven above.

You no longer walk about, but fly
Fuelled by compliments that flowed,
From your lover, this faultless one
Who all their love on you bestowed.

So your soaring heart glows bright,
Within your very soul and breast.
Marring sight and convincing you
That you'll pass your every test.

Your head will try hard to steer
A safe course of sense and welfare,
But your heart will not be cooled
From loves bright, saintly glare.

Dreams of wonder and dancing joy
Will swell into the heart and soul,
At the very sight of the one you love
Who makes the bells of Utopia toll.

For they can never do any wrong
And will love you all your years,
With their body, heart and kisses
And be your armour against all fears.

For you will think you know it all
With the fluttering thrill of love,
And the finding of your soul mate
Whose body fits you like a glove.

So walk in wonder, sun and light
Alongside your angel, who has fed
Your very breath, thought and being
That your heart rules, not your head!

--ooOoo--

Catching My Drift

At the crossroads I made my choice
And decided which road to choose,
Thus headed back towards your door
Believing that I had less to lose.

Split seconds make huge differences
Between success, or life and death.
But I could only hover and pray,
For a heartbeat, holding my breath!

My journey would make many turns
With both a heartache and elation,
At times I stopped, once turning back
Before arrival at my station,
Taking me quickly across the track
With trembling and pounding heart,
I knew that I was now almost there
So how would I play my part?

Would I laugh, smile, or even cry,
Perhaps to run, dawdle or crawl?
Major decisions, yet I was unsure
If I would make the last stop at all!

Split seconds make huge differences
Between success, or life and death.
But I could only hover and pray,
For a heartbeat, holding my breath!

I Believed that I still had my vote
On whether to proceed or run,
But I was really liked a trapped fly
Caught up in the web that was spun!

--ooOoo--

Laurie Wilkinson

The Nail and the Screw

The nail and the screw are different
But their function can be the same
Except for some slight make up,
Could be a rose by another name?

There are many people that you meet
Can be much like a nail or screw,
But your only way to be assured
Is to see how they'll treat you!

The screw will hold firm together
Surfaces needing to be held fast,
You can choose a large or small one
Depending how long it needs to last.

A nail's use can be much the same
If hammered into boards quite hard,
Again the nail size can be crucial
To ensure the finish isn't scarred.

Most screws are slow to enter
The pieces you want to secure.
Thus you have time to check up,
If holding tight and you are sure
That the screw is good and firm
And has entered true and straight,
Because if your aim is not correct
Your join won't take the weight!

Now the nail is much simpler
Just choose your size and hammer
Into the boards you need to fix,
Hitting cleanly with your rammer.
For if you hit the nail too hard
It may go in bent and not aligned,
And may not do the job too well
Or be just what you had in mind!

The nail and the screw are different
But their function can be the same,
Except for some slight make up,
Could be a rose by another name?

There are many people that you meet
Can be much like a nail or screw
But your only way to be assured
Is to see how they treat you.

For a "nail person" may be hard
And crash blindly into your world,
Reaching to the very soul of you
Before any agreement is unfurled!

The "screw character" may take time
Although see exactly what they do,
And even if you protest your pain
They may not care anything for you.

Thus if looking for your happy bond
You may need to compromise,
For with a screw person's slow pace
They can listen and be wordly wise.
Whilst the nail's determined force,
Perhaps a person with good intent
May just be able to consider first,
And do exactly what they meant!

--ooOoo--

Bridges

A bridge can join two sides up
But if destroyed keep them apart.
For if you need to cross a gorge
The bridge will help you start,
To bring a joining up as one
Separate sides of an argument.
So if bridging troubled waters
You may have a hearts content!

Some people burn their bridges
So they have no safe road back,
And if they need to turn around
They will realise what they lack.

For you may need to bridge build
If some offences you have caused,
To someone who you've let down
When affections you have paused.

A bridge can make a short cut
From a very long way around,
But before you put faith in it
Best ensure it's safe and sound,
Or you will learn the hard way
That quickest isn't always best.
And if that route's with people
Take great care to pass their test.

Like houses strong foundations
They're best built over time,
So bridges covering friendship
Must be sincere to be sublime.

For friends who last a lifetime
Will have had their rocky roads,
So the only way to survive this
Is with personal highway codes.

--ooOoo--

Second Look

The lady's looks were stunning
That every man would say,
But how will she deal with it,
When these looks all fade away?

Yes she was quite handsome
A very pretty sight to see,
But how will it affect her
Will she talk to you and me?

There are some attractive women
Who will always ring the bell,
But can they be all appropriate,
Or think they in heaven dwell?
So can act and be superior
And think they are god's gift,
Over staring fawning men folk
Whose gaze they cannot shift!

But I've known gorgeous women
So coy and down to earth,
Who treat everyone as equals
Proud of their humble birth.

The lady's looks were stunning
That every man would say,
But how will she deal with it
When these looks all fade away?

For attraction on the outside
Will soon fade, age and slide,
Past the easy to shine stage
For true beauty is from inside!

So the lovely but aloof lady
Will have to make a start,
To indulge and welcome all
As her looks soon fall apart.

--ooOoo--

Darkness

Some people don't like the dark
Others it just makes scared,
But there can be a comfort too
If all your soul you've bared.

Turning out the night time bulb
As if the power has all blown,
Can put you in a covering veil
Like in some protected zone.

Tired eyes will have their rest
And an aching body its ease,
So you can be lost in yourself
Where no one has the keys.

Many people cannot cope with this
It releases all their fears,
Some with recent broken hearts
Will collapse in flooding tears.
For any aching of the soul
Will damage the weak and brittle,
Leaving them knocked all about
Just as if they were a skittle.

But I can be at one with dark
So long as I have a beam,
To turn on if I feel the need
For I like my dark fed dream.

Laurie Wilkinson

These take away the daytime trials
Which can leave us all aggrieved,
Thus slipping into my warm dark
My soul will feel relieved.

--ooOoo--

Tiphaine

Like a coiled spring of laughter
That bursts across your face.
Lovely Tiphaine lifts your spirits,
Sinking dark clouds without trace.

And there's mischief behind the smile
That if ignored at your own choice,
You will certainly come to rue it
Regretting then, your lack of voice,
To challenge her witty humour
That will soon put you in retreat.
Being enchanted by the glamour
You are so very pleased to meet!

For there's no sides to our Tiphaine
She will always be the same,
And will only laugh the more
Should you beat her at her game
Of manic jokes and laughter,
That she really likes and enjoys.
And loves too your happy smiling
Even if you're one of the old boys.

So I have told her not to just settle
For the usual, ordinary track,
As with her humility and assets
To aim for stars and not look back!

--ooOoo--

Emergency Exit

When I needed love you gave it
Your mind and body too,
But I just couldn't break the chain
That was dividing me and you!

Though at any other time I'm sure
I would have run without a falter.
But my head and soul were crushed
So I had to commit the slaughter,
Of myself and a greater star
That had fallen joyous upon me.
For sometimes in a complex world
We are just too blind to see!

I needed love and you gave it
But how much I didn't know,
So when the emergency bell rang
I took the easiest route to go!

--ooOoo--

Grave Decision

There is no one at home
Because the door is locked.
No way in there for you
But are you really shocked?

Many times you tried to call
The phone just kept on ringing.
Mobile goes to answer phone,
No joy will that be bringing.

Of course you could send a text
She will never fail to see,
But still you get no reply
How obvious can it be?
You are in a contact ban
No interest in what you mutter,
It's far too late for you now
Whatever things you mutter!

Hasty words and decisions made
Without engaging the brain,
You can't go back and change it
So won't be the same again.

It's done then now you say
If that is how it lies,
You don't want a big drama
But you never said goodbyes.

Now everything's up in the air,
No clue to how it stands.
Though for you the music's gone,
No choir or marching bands.

Hasty words and decisions made
Without engaging the brain,
You can't go back and change it
So it won't be the same again.

It is said that wounds heal,
And every war will end.
But you know it's over now,
However much you pretend!

--ooOoo--

Promise for Tomorrow

Stunning, blazing, setting sun
Like a fireball in the sky,
Enriching even dismal views
Like a picnic for your eye.

It seems as if the day won't leave
Without an ending glorious sight,
Before it passes into dark
It has to demonstrate its might.
Then promise that it will be back,
With a shepherds delight tomorrow
So the day can slip away,
With cheer instead of sorrow.

Stunning, blazing setting sun
Like a fireball in the sky,
Enriching even dismal views
Like a picnic for your eye.

But be sure when night has done
And surrendered all the gloom,
The sun will come up once again
All keen to show its bloom.

Thus the shepherd will be right
About the promised daybreak,
So the only way to spoil the view
Is with bad decisions we make!

--ooOoo--

Laurie Wilkinson

HUMOUR

Laurie Wilkinson

Little Things

Our life is full of irritations
Yes, they're mostly just a glitch,
But if they all go wrong together
It really can make life a bitch!

Any time you're in a hurry
And you need to be out the door,
Then you'll knock something over
And watch it spread across the floor.

Something slips out of your fingers
So you bend to get it back,
Only then you see and realise
It's fallen through the smallest crack.

Liquid can be really tricky
As you determine not to spill,
But sure as eggs are eggs
It is certain that you will!
And not a little drop of liquid
However the amount you've got,
For when "Murphy" makes the rules
You will spill the flipping lot!

Our life is full of irritations
Yes, they're mostly just a glitch,
But if they all go wrong together
It really can make life a bitch!

My main hated little nuisance
That can make me lose my rag,
Is anything you're moving
Will be sure to catch or snag.

These small things sent to try us
Like the little "three foot judge",
Ensure when undoing something
It will determine not to budge.

I guess the most famous hate
Is when buttering some bread,
And knowing that if you drop it
It will land on the side that's spread.

Our life is full of irritations
Yes, they're mostly just a pain,
But if they all go wrong together
They can make you go insane!

One sad fact that is for certain
Is that if you get cross and sore,
Those little things that bug you
Will just happen more and more.

So perhaps the best salvation
Is to seek refuge in your bed,
But if "Murphy" has his way again
You will just fall out on your head!

--ooOoo--

Cocky Too's

Sitting on their bar stools
Just like parrots on a perch,
And delivering a sermon
As if they were in church.

Solving all the worlds deep problems
Without scarce a pause for breath,
It could be the beer talking
Or a latest script for meths!

My ears hear the words of wisdom
Spraying the bar room just like rain,
So I wonder why they're sat there
And driving everyone insane.

For if they have all the answers
To put all wrongs right,
Why not just go out and do it
And spare us all your sight!

Another correction to all errors
Follows a deep gulp of beer,
With a look that says i'm lucky
To be near enough to hear,
All the meaning of the mysteries
That world leaders cannot solve
Of poverty and pollution answers
That from this bar will evolve!

But I only went to the bar
To try to get myself a drink,
Past the barrier of "know all's"
That won't allow your brain to think
So I have my prudent answer
To the puzzle in my brain,
If I want peace and quiet
I won't come in here again!

--ooOoo--

Deposit Account

There is something in the toilet
That just won't go away,
Everyone can see it
But no one wants to say.

That this object just sits there
Looking very much like a log,
And somehow it remains
So you want to blame the dog,
For making this large deposit
In the urinal systems bank,
But wherever it came from
It's starting to smell rank.

Has someone not ate beans
Or taken tablets of iron?
Because it's getting nasty
And could now scare off a lion.

We've tried giving it a prod
And covering with some bleach,
Though it really is resistive
Like something beers can't reach.

But finally it goes away
And that's the end of that,
So now we will have to keep
A watch on the blooming cat!

Bears' Greatest Hits

Though Ted and Beth are travelling bears
Sometimes they stay home and rest,
And of all the things they love to do
Listening to music is their best.

Sometimes their Mum will play piano
And they will join in and sing,
About a teddies' picnic place
With lots of goodies they will bring.

Ted and Beth like other songs
Not just about teddy bears,
And one of their favourite ones is,
About a boy who climbs the stairs.

One Ted and Beth can't work out
That is about a strange bear,
Who in a garden walks round and round
And then tickles you under where???

Another song about a special bear
Whose name is Super Ted,
And I once heard Beth let slip
She would love him in her bed!

They also like pop videos too
With all the biggest hits,
Elvis, the Beatles and also Queen
And Madonna doing the splits!

But after a while all the songs
Just seem the same refrain,
So they start to get itchy paws
To be off travelling again!

--ooOoo--

All Wrapped Up

I can't open up the wrapper
No matter how hard I try.
Like undoing a peanut packet,
A big tug and out they fly!

Pull here, the packet glibly says
So there you pull but have no joy.
And the pouch stays firmly shut
As you pull and tug it like a toy.

Biscuits tightly wrapped are fun
When the opening tag won't work.
And the biscuits are now crumbs
As the packet you pull and jerk.

The cereal box says open here
So you dutifully aim to comply.
But hard luck, it's open other end,
So you just scream and cry!

Whatever type of wrapper cover
Is between you and your wares,
It will set up a conundrum test
Sure to give you bad nightmares.

If your goods don't have a tag pull
They'll be mummified all in tape,
That will hurt and break your nails
Leaving you with a puzzled gape.

So best be prepared for opening war
And arm yourself with all the tools,
Scissors, hammer, knife and bombs
For this package fight has no rules!

--ooOoo--

Chariot Wheels

Shopping trolleys are inanimate
I want to make that clear,
They really cannot be blamed
If pushed by a Boadicea

Waddling largies push these carts
Like Rommel with his tanks,
And should you be in line of attack
You must dodge with little thanks.

Whether you are in or out the store
The dangers just the same,
Except inside there is little room
And much less chance to complain.

Outside in the widespread terrain
Your worry is their speed,
Or the lack of route or direction
So look out or you will bleed!

Propelled with gusto by the hulks
They roar across the road,
And doesn't need a genius to see
They don't know the Highway Code.

The shopping trolley chariot race
Should fill your heart with fear,
For driven by these Amazon's
Even Ben Hur would not go near!

So stepping back inside the shop
You should feel no need to beg,
Until an unseeing Genghis Khan
Shoves their trolley in your leg.

Little old ladies are just as bad
And be sure you are no freer,
For they've no idea where to push,
And you they can't see or hear.

These rattling supermarket trains
That is the shoppers trolley,
In themselves are little threat
Only when trundled by a wally,
Of whom there seems to be a horde
Not knowing where their going,
And don't see or care for us
Who risk all by our unknowing.

That to survive the trolley dash
You must forget all manners,
And do your very best to avoid
Trolley chariots and their banners!

--ooOoo--

Mr. Splash

I call myself mister splash
And I just really cannot stop,
For however careful that I am
I always spill things with a plop.

Not like I'm dropping everything
More of a sort of splash about,
Like wielding a watering can
When I always drop the spout.

Any nicely rubbed clean surface
All cleared and wiped down dry,
Will soon be wet and soaking
When a tap jet makes water fly.

I can brew a lovely cup of tea
Even coffee I make well too,
But when walking to take it out
Then it will slop all on my shoe.

Washing up is nice and easy
And one of my usual chores,
But whilst all the cups are clean
There's water all on the floors.

Pouring water from the kettle
Into the cups and saucers there,
Often makes a messy splash
That makes me cuss and swear.

Taking tea bags from the cups
And to put out into the waste,
Will always splat on the table
As I drop them in my haste.

So I'm trying hard to be good
And not splash stuff everywhere,
By slowing myself down a bit
Will help me take more care!

--ooOoo--

Music Hall

I just love listening to my music
There's some on most of the time,
From Mozart through to hard rock
For me, all types of music's fine.

Obviously there are some times
When a certain music's plays best,
Some you want to jump about to
While classic's can help you rest.

For ballroom dancing there's some,
That help you keep with the beat.
Blues and folk may have a story,
Rock can make you tap your feet!

Middle of the road stuff, like Abba
Make you sing and dance together.
Hymn's and carols mark the season,
Travel music recalls great weather.

All music styles and types are fine
And most make your fingers tap.
But there is one none music dud,
That is the banging, chanting Rap!

Stuttering mad like a machine gun,
Vocals spat out in repetitive spite.
I have gone with punk and protest,
But to me, angry rap's not right!

St st still it t t takes all music tastes
And this rap clap is tasting rotten.
So unlike Johnny R of the Pistols
This rap clap will soon be forgotten.

Give me The Beatles or The "Stones"
The Who, Small Faces, Buddy Holly.
A Mozart opera, a fine Strauss waltz,
All of these can soon make me jolly.

Even Elvis rocking with shaking hips,
Country and Western's cowboy dance.
Moody Blues, Queen, and The Move,
Even Johnny Hallyday from France!

So many more music stars and themes,
Sinatra, Cliff Richard, lots of girls too,
Don't forget musicals, Les Mis and Cats.
These will all thrill and entertain you.

Thus we're lucky with our music types,
Have a good look and make your choice.
Whatever you fancy, just take your pick,
From lovely classic's, to beautiful voice.

But just do me one great favour please,
Don't play rap anywhere near my ears!
Almost anything else fills me with glee,
The rap clap I just drown with beers!

--ooOoo--

Barely Heard

Ted and Beth are very happy
Content bears and not bores,
But there is a little problem
Beth has told me that Ted snores!

Ted of course he denies this
And says it's just not true.
Though actually I heard him,
Only that's between me and you.

Beth says she is quite desperate
To have a peaceful night.
For every time she drops off,
Ted's snort gives her a fright.

He says it's all an exaggeration
That many male bear's growl,
But Beth is getting very angry,
And may smother him with a towel.

There has to be a solution to,
This noise that comes from Ted.
For Beth states if it continues
He must sleep in the spare bed!

So that's the way they managed
With no arguments, no pain.
Until both of them got lonely,
And had to sleep together again.

Once more they are contented
Though Ted still makes a noise,
So Beth wears some ear plugs
Because he's best of Teddy boys!

--ooOoo--

Beware the Unaware

I'm glad people are not motor cars
There would be crashes every day,
For even if you are walking straight
Someone walks out in your way!

It's clear there's not a highway code
For pedestrians out on the street.
Because however much you dodge
They will tread hard on your feet.

Coming straight out from the shop
People do not glance up or look,
And walk right out in front of you
Whatever avoidance tack you took.

Stop and starting, a turn left or right
No one bothers to look all around.
So they emergency stop unaware,
Another person is collision bound!

Trolleys, prams, mobility buggies,
The three monkey's driving it seems.
Not so wise, and no hearing or seeing,
Circling around, lost in their dreams.

People on mobile phones, unaware,
Stepping out and not looking at all.
It's amazing that they don't trip up,
Or walk unsighted right into a wall!

Walkers striding with ear pieces in,
Can't hear even if you were a coach.
But that doesn't seem to deter them,
They are oblivious to any approach.

So every day we run the human race,
With no rules in the great walkabout.
Thus there is bumping and pushing,
And all your fault without a doubt!

--ooOoo--

No Entry

There's a gremlin in my lap top
Who reads my every word,
And causes little glitches
Whilst I have hardly stirred.

It sits watching all my typing
So when the last word is near,
There is a flicker on the screen
And my work will all disappear.

Now any attempt to retrieve it
Makes gremlin laugh and scoff,
For each time I touch the panel
He turns the damn thing off!

Though I have a perfect signal
And connection speed is great,
Still my little Genie gremlin
Says my "save as" was too late.

Now my full battery sign is on
So all's well, and off I go,
To try to get the work back
But my reaction time is slow.

So I need to start off thinking
What can this gremlin be?
But I have an uneasy feeling
It is all blooming down to me!

--ooOoo--

Locked Out

Knock went the door, ring ring the bell
Or not as the case would be,
We are in the cold and stuck outside
But don't worry it's just little me!
Though that fact is not totally true
There was Jo and John outside too,
Yes it was odd and a mystery
But the thing was a lot worse for me,
The others were miffed, and in the cold
I just wanted a wee!

Then came the others to join us
They were invited there too,
I won't say that we would riot
But not only the air was blue!
Even the neighbours saw us,
Have you moved in they asked?
No, none of us live here,
But getting in seems like a task!

We banged on the door really loudly
Enough to awaken the dead.
When all of a sudden you stood there
Bewildered you looked up and said,
I did not think you were coming,
And we thought you were in bed!
But at last we gained entry
And a lovely evening ensued,
But to leave guests out freezing
Is not something to be pursued!

--ooOoo--

Naked Ambition

The shower setting at the gym
Is a place for communal undress,
With all kinds of behaviour
But perhaps some you should guess.

You can see all the different types
By their various mannerisms there.
For some are quite shy and bashful,
But others just stand and stare!

There is though one unwritten code
Whether you smile or wear a frown.
It says you can do much as you like
But you never ever look down.

Though some it doesn't seem to faze
They swagger like a smiling punk.
I'm sure it wouldn't matter to them,
If they had a finger, or a trunk!

Others creep quickly out the shower,
A private person you'd have guessed.
It's possible that they're very quiet
Or else not been well blessed.

The kingpin though, a man of brawn
Absolute content with what he's got.
But catching a glance in a mirror
It was surprisingly not a lot!

As for me with my large sized mouth,
I'm just happy to laugh with those.
Who also have no reason to brag,
But you'd not like it on your nose!

--ooOoo--

Front Line Action

I don't want a pot belly
They say it comes with age.
Looking at some younger folk,
It seems they're all the rage!

Is it the booze that causes it,
Or eating fast food "take aways"?
But whatever the reason for it,
Should you get a "pot", it stays.

It's said that if you eat too much
The weight goes to your tum.
But I think that's only half of it,
It's also sitting idle on your bum!

Few people want to walk much
So they stand at the taxi rank,
Or drive just a few yards or so
In a giant motor, like a tank.

I don't like my pot that's there
Just above my trouser line.
But I must admit to feeling smug,
If they're over twice the size of mine.
And back sides too, are getting big,
In those outsize clothes they pack
Those very large and active cheeks,
Like two pigs playing in a sack!

So it's food, drink and sitting down
Too much, that all causes growth.
With lots of people waddling round,
Having one big leg the size of both.

But one thing has come to our aid
In the shape of big electric carts,
That carry heavyweights around
With all of their outsized parts!

--ooOoo--

Threadbear Cover

Ted and Beth like being stars
And not only featured in a book,
But also in a national paper
So real posers now they look.

Ted's taken to wearing dark glasses
He thinks they make him look cool,
But Beth just laughs back at him
Saying he looks a right Teddy fool!

Mind you, Beth likes her fame too,
Talking to her friends on the phone.
Saying about being a "poem star"
And thinking she was home alone.

But Ted and Beth know their lucky
Having such a great life for bears,
With their fun, fame and travels
As they enjoy life without any cares!
Though they are always asking me
What I will tell about them next?
So I say, just behave yourselves
Or I will write you out of context!

Now I believe that three new poems
On them, in this poetry book closed.
Is enough as although they're bears
I don't want them too over exposed!

--ooOoo--

REFLECTION

All or Something

Life is a feast or famine
And never seems to even out,
Either all the land is flooding
Or we're suffering a drought.

If you want to catch a bus
You are standing like a dunce,
Past your final waiting time
Then four will come at once!

Luck seems to be the same
You will get every call right,
Then quickly as it changes
You lose everything in sight.

Getting your finances done
Bills paid with money left,
When a run of expenses come
And all at once you are bereft.

Fishermen cast their bait
And the nets are filled tight,
But then there is a long time
With not one single bite.

Life is feast or famine
And never seems to even out,
Either all the world is flooding
Or we're suffering a drought.

Is it a game that's played
By angels and mascots creed?
That allows a win sometimes
Before stopping all our greed.

Perhaps it's our perception
Of what we want to obtain.
But whatever does befall us
We must get back up again!

--ooOoo--

Hearsay

Our lives can be very complex
As we wend our weary way,
So we may feel the need to talk
But must watch what we say.

For candid talk can be dangerous
If life turns on its head,
And you may very much regret
Some words that you have said.
About a person, place or thing
You genuinely felt was right,
And if twisted or misconstrued
They can come back to bite.

For times will change for certain
With opinions of past themes,
So when your words are called back
It could be nightmares and not dreams.

For candid talk can be dangerous
If life turns on its head,
And you may very much regret
Some words that you have said.

So on our intrepid trip of life
With many a pitfall or bend,
Without intent or fault of yours
You may lose a confided friend.

And repeat of your spoken thoughts
May not come out like yours did,
So more innocence that you protest
Will only further lift the lid!

Thus an angry friend or lady scorned
May just come back to bite,
And people love to see the worst,
Even if you're in the right..

For candid talk can be dangerous
If life turns on its head,
And there is little you can do now
If some people cut you dead.

So the conundrum that is life
Poses who to speak to first?
For if you keep in all your words
Your troubled brain may burst!

--ooOoo--

Open Up

I'm so glad that I spoke to you
How else would I have known,
Thoughts that you have told me
That are all you very own?

You shared just what you think
What makes you laugh or cry,
The things that make you angry,
That you love, or perhaps let by.

We can often pass each other
Without a smile or spoken word,
And that we don't talk to each other
Is quite frankly so absurd!

We need to share our feelings
And how others may endure.
For in a world of madness
It's good to know what's pure.
By listening and talking
We learn some different views,
Like how life can be for others
When before we had no clues.

We can often pass each other
Without a smile or spoken word,
And that we don't talk to each other
Is quite frankly so absurd!

So give a nod, or even smile
Who knows what may pan out?
You may have great times spent
If you end your speaking drought!

--ooOoo--

Altered Lives

Facebook farms out people's lives
And all that folk want to say,
Of wonder felt and places seen
Like how you've had the greatest day.

You can type and post at your will
And put each very latest photo in,
A broad smiling chap drinking beer
Who is always miserable as sin!

For mostly we are led to believe
That your loving soul mate is best,
Yet strangely when you talk alone
You say that you're not really blessed.

Wonder kids with mammoth brains
Their parents are so very proud,
Before the super child's prize is won
A success is shouted right out loud!
So some other mere mortals tell me
That they feel so inferior and sad,
Because no future brilliant child
Star of theirs, have they got or had!

Private dirty linen is all hung out,
For the worlds sympathy or shame
On unfortunate ex partners or spouse
Who must surely take all the blame.

But wait, for I must take some flak
For the content of some of my posts,
That I purposely put on to tweak
And wind up those superstar hosts.

Who bring on the need for vomit bags
And cause normal minds to grieve,
But not so many are easily taken in
For their magic lives we don't believe!

But of course like any other system
Facebook can make you laugh or frown,
Especially through it's worldwide web
A dear lost friend it helps track down!

--ooOoo--

Doorstop

A door can be unpleasant
If shut right in your face,
Or closed tight and daunting
To most of the human race.

For if solid you won't see in
At scenes played right inside,
Allowing secrecy of actions
That insiders want to hide!

Doors literally go both ways
And can keep you safely in,
Protecting you and property
From those out to commit sin,
Or allow yourself some space
And the privacy you need,
From those unwanted callers
Who "don't disturb" won't read.

But shut doors aren't sealed
As a key can work the lock.
If you want to give access in,
To folk without their knock!

So a door can be friend or foe
Depending on mood or need,
Like locking it to strangers
Who may only enter for greed.

Whilst you can happily open
Your door to someone dear,
That you will always welcome
As you know they are sincere!

--ooOoo--

Tango for One

They say it takes two to tango
And you must have two to dance.
But I don't fully agree with this,
As alone you can make your stance!

For you are mostly responsible for,
Any bad things that happen to you.
And whilst it's easy to blame others,
It's largely down to what you do.
With any recorded success or not
And your choices of people met,
So any failure or unwanted grief
Is all down to your bad call or bet!

They say it takes two to tango
And you must have two to dance.
But I don't fully agree with this,
As alone you must take your stance.

Though it's nice to dance with another
Who makes all your troubles seem small.
But don't be fooled it will last forever,
As it's all your fault should you stall!

--ooOoo--

The Easy Life

We take our life for granted
So easy to talk the talk,
But have you ever imagined
A life if you can't walk?

Many get by in a wheelchair
Showing tremendous courage too,
But however you look at it
Tasks are twice as hard to do.

Everything we accept as usual
So simple for you and me,
Like using a public toilet
But disabled need a key!

Having a meal round a table,
We do it most every day.
But if sat there in a wheelchair,
You may feel in the way.
Whilst disabled do not choose it,
Doing most things is a chore,
Trying to navigate our pavements,
Or even opening a door.

Lots of folk have no understanding
Of how disability is involved,
With complications of movement
However determinedly resolved.

Add compromise of privacy
With independence reduced,
These make many life restrictions
Just however they're deduced!

So perhaps for best comprehension
Go round in a wheelchair for a day,
And without doubt you will realise,
You can't moan or feel dismay!

--ooOoo--

Write or Wrong?

Not everyone is good at spelling
It's a sort of gift or art,
But there is no need for failure
As you can check it from the start.

In any heartfelt publication
Or a note or a letter penned,
Will lose respect or meaning
Unless spell check time you spend.

We have a fine but complex language
But don't spell words as they sound,
So it's really quite important
That mistakes you make are found.
Before you post or send them
For lots of people to peruse
At your words and read them
For if wrong, they may confuse!

In any heartfelt publication
Or a note or letter penned,
Will lose respect or meaning
Unless spell check time you spend.

Another pitfall in our writing
Is that little apostrophe,
Flagging possession or omission
Used wrong it's not good to see.

So before your writing flourishes
You must check you've got it right,
For any bad or careless error
Will diminish your pen's might!

--ooOoo--

Framed

Staring out from inside a frame
Your smiling, happy scene.
Captured in that photograph
To prove where you have been!

Could it be a tranquil time
Frozen there from your past?
Lovely days, a fleeting sight
You hoped would always last.

For pictured in that photo flash
A scene that didn't take too long,
But will stay and show for ever
So can never say what's wrong,
If the memory was questioned
About how it all turned out,
Over times that rolled on slowly
That photo may cause a doubt!

So a perfect shot of instant flash
That may not show what's right,
But preserved now in that frame
Is a nice image of perfect sight!

--ooOoo--

Laurie Wilkinson

The Farmer and the Magpie

The farmer works ploughing fields
And scatters good seed around,
The Magpie will not do a stroke
But takes all that can be found.

The farmer's day starts at early dawn
And he works hard all year long,
The Magpie will take from everyone
Not thinking they've done wrong.

For it seems to some people in our life
They can give no bean nor clout,
So the more that they see you put in
That bit extra they take out!

The parable of the Talents
Tells of the man who wasted
All that he was given then,
Took yours you'd not yet tasted.

So our farmer works his boots off
To provide for him and friends,
Whilst the Magpie looks slyly on
Then just squanders more, and spends.
Not thinking of the workload
That farming types put in,
But for our opportunist thief
Such a commitment is a sin!

It must be some strange attitude
That allows the thief to thrive,
Off the back of others work
Like the farmer's gathered hive.

But all this doesn't matter
To our thieving Magpie's gains,
For not a jot or care has he
For ours or the farmer's pains!

--ooOoo--

Laurie Wilkinson

Better or Worse

The years that pass will change us all
For many better ways, some worse.
Struggling through life's many trials
We will be tested, chapter and verse.

People we meet in life may cheat
And not turn out as we perceived,
But if we challenge or call them out
They'll protest, and be aggrieved.
For we've not measured up for them
All they needed to take from us,
Thus we must stand there as accused
Denied speech, or to make a fuss!

So the time that's passing changes all
But if faltering we can be condemned.
Though our good points are overlooked
And our errors we did not amend.

Many disputes are caused by love
And disagreements as to who is best.
So friendships that stood many years
Will struggle to survive this test!

If someone once close can succeed
When your friend and mate just fails,
A jealousy and sourness may arise
As friendship poisoned, just derails.

Our money is a tricky source of change
When wasted, stolen, lost or gained.
For everyone could make their pile
And those who didn't, say they refrained
To take the opportunities that they had
Because to achieve all is so simple,
But of course didn't take their chance
So hate disfigures, like a rash or pimple.

Thus life will salute all those who stand
Unbeaten, without change, so sincere,
Through all ravages of life upon them.
But maybe not so good as they appear.
For little temptations may have wrought
Some small dents in their gold exterior!
And denied too vigorously if not true
Prove that they actually are inferior!

--ooOoo--

People Places

People and places from your past
Are no longer there, or the same.
So will make you notice more
The years you couldn't tame.

People known from distant days
Maybe won't still be around.
So you must indulge old friends
Before you too run aground!

Places where you knew each stone
Will now soon lose you in a trice,
And even finding a familiar part
Will still make you look twice,
Because memories will play tricks
On what you thought you knew,
And many a place or person now
Seems different from your view.

People known from distant days
Maybe won't still be around.
So you must indulge old friends
Before you too run aground!

So going back where you've been
May not be for the very best,
As these places may disturb you
If they've not survived times test.

But people are somewhat different
Always worth a nostalgic greet,
For though they may have changed
It will be good for you to meet,
And share those long gone times
Where you both ran alongside,
Each other with your experiences
From which you should not hide!

--ooOoo--

Brash Banned

The small minded person says a lot
And whilst smiling must be brash,
Shouting out they speak their mind
But if challenged they'll soon crash.
For to give out insults and be smart
You have to be strong like a stack.
And also prepared to accept grief,
If others words come straight back!

I was always taught to share a joke
And bandy humour off like a spout.
But the massive lesson of this game,
Is to take what you have given out!

Sadly some people don't get this fact
And bellow out just what they feel.
But should you dare to criticise them
They soon moan and start to appeal.
For mostly these crass people brag
In a hypocrite's way of getting by.
Believing they've the right to abuse,
But on the receiving end they'll cry.

I was always taught to share a joke
And bandy humour off like a spout.
But the massive lesson of this game
Is to take what you have given out!

So we can see their spiteful words
They aim cowardly at all other folk.
Never to see the humour or irony,
That upset they'll whinge and choke.

--ooOoo--

Laurie Wilkinson

Round Trip

Time moves on and passes by
As I look back down the years,
To see good times and heartache
But a lot more fun than tears.

We can't always control our lives
And why our world has cracked,
But your manner and character
Are judged by how you react!

So looking back with a sadness
At the times you regret or lost,
Will only waste and frustrate
Time you already want to accost.

Thus best to count your blessings
And good things that you've got,
For even if you're struggling by
To many others you'll have a lot.

Time moves on and passes by
As I look back down the years,
To see good times and heartache
But a lot more fun than tears.

Of course trials and tribulations
Can easily make you go insane.
But when I'm due to pass away,
Please can I go round again?

Home Comforts

You must really count your blessings
I do that each and every day,
For there's always someone worse off
No matter what you think or say!

We live closely in our own world
So don't see much else around,
And very little effects us here
Thus we sleep safe and sound.

No war now overshadows us
Earthquake, drought or heavy weather.
In fact if we get deep heavy snow
There's panic running hell for leather!

We have no major killing diseases
Of course cancer threatens us all,
But that's a worldwide problem too
Thus our health concerns are small.

Well apart that is from obesity
That will be the new fatal killer,
Unless people stop eating fast food
And go easy on their stomach filler.

We live closely in our own world
So don't see much else around,
And very little effects us here
Thus we sleep safe and sound.

So rest safely in your beds tonight,
For it's only you that cause distress
And shockwaves in your tranquil pond,
Thus why would we settle for less!

--ooOoo--

Recall

Ghosts from our early life
May come back to haunt,
Playing down the fun times
While bad days they'll flaunt.

So how best to deal with this
Recall of past days and years?
Being morbid wishing for change
And spending your future in tears?

Far better to learn from times
You made the wrong bet or call.
Indulging days that you enjoyed
With good prospects and no squall!

--ooOoo--

TRAGEDY

After Life

What becomes of the bereaved?
And how do they cope with loss.
After all the initial arrangements,
With sad goodbyes beneath a cross.

The home you shared is silent now
And your footsteps echo loud.
But there is no one there to tell
You now live beneath a cloud,
Of painful sadness, loss and tears
And no companion of many years,
Who often made you hopping mad
But the best friend you'd ever had!

The family do care but are so busy
Trying to keep their world intact.
And though they phone or call in,
Your strong resolve has cracked.

What becomes of the bereaved?
And how do they cope with loss.
After all the initial arrangements,
With sad goodbyes beneath a cross.

So who can see all your inner pain?
And take away the hurt and ache,
Of missing someone once so close
That you force each move you make.

You never thought you'd be alone
Thinking you would leave earth first.
But life never pans out as you think
So these fears are all your worst!

Then slowly, softly you come to terms
With acute loneliness and still.
While some people avoid you now,
You're crushed by your empty chill.

So what does become of the bereaved?
When no one knows just what to say.
While your world empties and narrows
As you just try to fill each day!

--ooOoo--

Break Down

There is a silent lonely shadow
That reflects the broken man.
His world has crashed completely
And his last bit of courage ran,
Very slowly in life's gutter,
And trickled down the drain.
Now however much he struggles,
It just won't come back again.

What has caused this disaster,
And brought him down to this?
Was it a lover's betrayal,
The giving of a Judas kiss?
Or merely that the world
Seemed to turn on him alone.
Well that's how he is feeling
And chilled right to the bone.

There may be lots of reasons
That can all pull a man apart,
Maybe a face he knew so fully
Is now missing in his heart?
Or could it be so very simple,
As to why he looks so old?
A love that was so steamy,
Has now turned icy cold?

Was it a family bereavement,
A friend or business lost?
For it now haunts his features
And makes him count the cost,
Of getting off his fence,
And trying much too hard.
Maybe giving all his love
Or just lowering his guard.

But whatever caused his drama
Or how much he feels the pain,
The world will keep on turning
And not see him go insane!
Now the weather forecast is good
And the sun will be shining bright,
But now it only will bring shadows
Across his tortured inner plight!

--ooOoo--

Stain of Shame

Near three thousand went to work
Though none would make it back,
They would all be the victims
Of a sick cowardly attack.

Without any warning from the skies
And two huge towers did remove.
Though left a bigger stain of shame,
Of which no god could approve.

Many a madman in history charged
With a massive sword a wielding,
But it takes a special psychotic mind
To steer planes into a building!

A tremor was felt across humanity
We knew that evil had been done,
But their bitter, sickly souls were less,
Than their smoke that hid the sun.

Near three thousand went to work
Though none would make it back,
They would all be the victims
Of a sick, cowardly attack.

With towers burning there is no escape
Trapped up high from crowds around,
The only choice was manner of death
To burn, choke, or hit the ground.

There was time though, with technology
For tragic folk to phone their kin,
And heartrending love and goodbyes
Only compound their killer's sin.

They said the world couldn't be the same
After this cruel act of desecration,
But the spirit of good and righteousness
Is built on a very strong foundation.

Near three thousand went to work
Though none would make it back,
They would all be the victims
Of a sick, cowardly attack.

So time has passed into history now
That blackest day of days.
The world moves on now as it must,
But contempt and disgust still stays,

For those whose simplistic minds
Were twisted to an act of hate,
Upon unsuspecting innocents
Who walked like heroes to their fate!

--ooOoo--

Laurie Wilkinson

Deep Rooted

Sometime in life will come your test
It may come early, or near your end.
So even the lucky will have to pause,
While their shattered heart they mend.

But rest assured though a test is hard
It will instil in you a heart of oak,
And although you retain your charity
Your laws of life, will not revoke.
For you will have a sound, hard spirit
That you know now can't be wrought,
Because you stood firm as others fell
Thus your inherent lesson was taught!

Sometime in life will come your test
It may come early, or near your end.
So even the lucky will have to pause,
While their shattered heart they mend.

I look back to regard my test in life
When my world crashed all around,
And for some time I floundered lost
Until my proud stoic root I found.
So whenever life became a trial
I knew that somehow I'd succeed.
And overcome the hardship or pain,
For my deep rooted spirit would lead!

--ooOoo--

The Sad Man

The sad man strives to be the best,
Well that is what he hopes.
But his heavy heart can never rest,
That is why he always mopes.

He closely watches others gains
To compare and check himself,
For he fears that if not the brains
He will be left back on the shelf!

Not noticing others self content
Who work and live with pleasure.
The sad man just cannot relent
Watching how well he'll measure.

For standing out and shining bright
Matters more in life to him.
And yearning for a glowing light
Just makes him look more dim.

He closely watches others gains
To compare and check himself,
For he fears that if not the brains
He will be left back on the shelf!

But climbing up the tree of life
Can leave the sad man tired,
With no joys and only strife
He will have very soon expired!

Game to Lose

Your game of life is often played
In front of the watching crowd,
Who see your each and every move
As you stand small, or very proud.

So the fence sitters will only watch
How others cope with their game.
And decrying all those who've lost
Whilst jealous of the victors fame.

For if you won't take a part in life
You can deride and mock at will,
All those who try to do their best
To enjoy life, and so they'll fulfil.

So that's why I have strongly felt
It's far better to have tried and lost.
For if you won't compete or try
You'll much later count your cost,
Of just cowardly sitting at the side,
Never taking any risk or chance.
Making you a lonely, boring case,
And not worth a second glance!

But by getting stuck in having a go
It's just possible you may win out.
And that must be so much better
Than not to know a winners shout.

So our cosy spectators of the world
Will always rue not being brave,
And missed the warmth of joining in
Thus taking a sadness to their grave!

--ooOoo--

Last Dance Lesson

You have danced your last on earth
No more to feel the rhythms true,
Though some will mourn your passing
As they never got to dance with you.

For dancing is a life expression
Your own personality and style,
Not just moves on a dance floor
But what makes you laugh or rile.

So if people missed your steps
And what you were all about,
They will never get to know now
Thus must look back with doubt.
Why they didn't share with you
Gifts and humour that were unique,
So they've missed that awareness
However hard now they may seek.

Our dance on earth is precious,
Better if you share the beat
For the tango must have two,
So you may rue your retreat
Into sorrow for waltz or rumba
You will now have to do alone,
As you denied yourself a partner
Due to your heavy heart of stone.

For dancing is a life expression
Your own personality and style,
Not just moves on a dance floor
But what makes you laugh or rile.

Thus the band has nearly finished
And the dancing almost through,
So we must make our sacrifices
For who dances last with you!

--ooOoo--

Last Request

Tears of frustration and anguish
Drip slowly from your eye,
You can't do things like you used to
So maybe you just want to die?

It is easy to say your time is done
You wish you would breathe no more,
But just as you're thinking hard on this
Another soul fights to avoid deaths door.

But you have pains and living is hard
Everything's changed, your importance less,
So you would like to sleep the long sleep,
Until you are faced with the final distress.

You awake depressed how life turned out
And you should have done so much better.
So you feel very sad and your body aches,
Much simpler to be free from the fetter.

It is easy to say your time is done
You wish you would breathe no more,
But just as you are thinking hard on this
Another soul fights to avoid deaths door.

You feel and say you would like to be gone
And ask "O death were is thy sting?"
It appeals to consider your very last day,
Until down the final curtain they bring!

Then there is panic, you're not quite so sure,
Just what awaits at the end of that road?
And so you quickly count all your blessings,
With all the love that to you was bestowed.

So maybe you should give life another go,
You really didn't mean what you said.
For being confronted by the final frontier,
Will fill every one with cold dread!

For it's so easy to say your time is done
And you wish you could breathe no more.
Then just while you're thinking hard on this,
You are pushed through your deaths trap door!

--ooOoo--

Sumo Story

The gentleman was extremely fat
Nothing else that you could say,
But the most concerning thing
Was that he got bigger every day.

The kids would always taunt him
Wherever he was or tried to go,
And it really hurt and upset him
When they called out, "hey Sumo"!

But he wasn't always like this
So overweight and out of trim.
In fact he'd been very handsome,
With big muscles, and quite slim.

So we must ask what's happened
To let himself go such as this?
Well there is much more to it
But it all started with a kiss,
With a girl who took him over,
His heart, his soul, his mind.
In fact he fell for her completely,
But to him she was so unkind.

Our man though, couldn't see it
He thought she was "the one",
That he'd love and spend his life with
But he was about to come undone!

She took him for every penny
And also cheated on him too.
When he finally asked her why?
She told him just what he could do!

Having seen her take all his money,
And trample on his self respect.
He just could not cope with it,
And thus began his self neglect.

His only comfort became his food
And he didn't work out any more.
He just kept on with his eating
Until weighing twenty stone and four!

His friends had tried to help him
But he only retreated with his feast.
And ignored all the pleas of others
Turning into a very angry beast.

Thus the man the kids called Sumo
Has lost everything he once had.
And now the world can't help him
So he is just lonely, fat and sad.

But our mister Sumo was aware
Of what would likely be his fate,
So he decided that he'd beat it
With a rope that took his weigh!

--ooOoo--

Locked Inside

Every one of us is afraid
At some time in our life
From small daily interactions
To more daunting tasks and strife.

We walk lost among the majesty
And wonders of our world,
But there's hidden doubts and fears
That just want to be unfurled.

And these many uneasy feelings
That start to push and probe,
Can explode our inner secrets
Like a shattered precious globe.

Causing self doubt and foreboding
That there must be something wrong,
With what we've said or stand for,
So any peace can't last for long.

For insecurities and paranoia
Will grow large and drown our mood,
As we batter down our hatches
So dormant shadows don't intrude.

Others silence or covert laughter
Must all be aimed at us,
Seeming to look right inside
Our trembling souls, with little fuss.

So stand firm, proud and defiant
At this deep inner scrutiny,
And have the courage to roar loudly
That what you see inside is me!

--ooOoo--

Laurie Wilkinson

Stolen

I wish that I could talk to you
There is so much I want to say,
As I was never given a chance
When you were stolen away.

Oh why do the very best of us
Get taken at such an early time?
As the "never do wells" live on,
You hardly got to your prime!

You had done so much for me
Perhaps not seen until too late,
But how was I to ever guess
You'd soon be at heavens gate?

I wanted so much to thank you
And to tell you all my news,
About the things I was doing,
For all your advice and views.

I wish that I could talk to you
There is so much I want to say,
As I was never given a chance
When you were stolen away.

But that was a long time ago
There is so much now to share.
So I would love to sit and talk

But I know that you're not there,
To laugh and joke beside me
As you kindly put me straight,
On the things that I got wrong,
For you were my closest mate!

--ooOoo--

Loves Departure

Your angel of love has now departed
So you are left here sad and alone,
By the one you hoped you'd die with
Who you placed on your hearts throne.

No more miracle of loves perfection
Will be there to love and walk beside,
As you lurch blindly through the days
You know something deep has died!

And with this death of your feelings
You see the spectre that's your heart,
Rot like a corpse that lies unburied
And your numb soul is ripped apart.

Limping through the world of sorrow
You hear the life spectators mock,
For you cannot find rhyme or reason
As you stare blankly, still in shock!

Thinking that love was to last forever
Whatever else was to be said or done,
For those promises now echo falsely
So now your nightmares just begun.

You look back at those good times,
And all that you happily sacrificed.
Now washed up as shipwreck waste
That through your heart has sliced.

So now you trudge your tearful journey
Of life, that you must make all alone.
No more those glorious, bright horizons,
Just black shadow and a heart of stone!

--ooOoo--

The Voice Within

When all alone or robbed of sleep
Deepest fears will leave their mark,
You cannot hide, there's no escape
From that voice loud in the dark.

You tremble, shiver, toss and turn,
And inner secrets are laid bare.
No pleading, or screwed tight eyes,
Can escape that haunting glare.

For this deep searching voice within
That you really can't ignore,
And try your hardest not to hear
Will sear right to your core.

We all have deep insecurities
Or worries we just can't park.
So at our most unguarded times,
This voice creeps from the dark.

You tremble, shiver, toss and turn,
And inner secrets are laid bare.
No pleading, or screwed tight eyes,
Can escape the haunting glare.

You shut your ears, blink the eyes,
Do the best to gird your loins.
But you really have no protection,
So you split open at the joins!

But when you come apart it's clear
What this deep fear will find.
For awakened by the creeping voice,
Is the conscience of your mind!

--ooOoo--

Final Destination

As we near our final destination
Where the dead are gathered in,
Some will be heavy hearted
Others reflecting on each sin.

But there's no need to be saintly
And do lots of good with charm,
You only have to worry
If your failings have caused harm.

For things are not all cut and dried
In the land of the Reaper Grimm,
As many a haunted lost soul
Will gladly run to him!

So as we near our final destination
Where the dead are gathered in,
Some will be heavy hearted
Others reflecting on each sin.

Yes, getting at our journey's end
Can be a very long, hard road,
And with aching, weary bones
It seems you have a growing load.

And as tricks of life are played out
So some stutter, hurt and fall,
Looking painfully round at others
Who much older, still stand tall!

So as we reach our final destination
With some fresh as opening day,
Well, they look that on the outside
But in truth they never got to play.

So we're running down and counting
How many days that remain,
And the victor is easily spotted
Trying hard to start off again!

--ooOoo--

Loss of Life

The game of life is sliding away
Whatever path you're choosing,
Of different style, or tactic tried,
The cold fact is you're losing.

There's a bad an sickening feeling
That chills you through and through,
When you realise you can't win
No matter what you try to do!

Life will have all the answers
On whichever call you make,
All is slipping through your fingers,
And it is more than you can take.

So you try to change yourself,
Maybe how you are perceived.
But it only leaves frustration,
And a sense you've been deceived.

Now you're staring at more failure
Feeling the lowest of the low,
But you just can't win anything
Despite how much you know.

Thus in desperation you stand still
Scared to take one more chance,
Until life has finally left you
Without a pause or second glance!

Appendix

Feedback on my poetry recounts that many people like to work out the meanings of my poems for themselves and even attach their own personal experiences and thoughts. I think that is wonderful, but for other people who like to seek my explanations please review my comments below.

As I tend to write spontaneously and often on subjects that have emoted me, most of the themes are self explanatory. The poems in this appendix are less obvious themes, but feel free to add any personalisation as to how the poems are for you individually.

A Wildest Dream	A defeated love
Eye Line Smile	Poem on love
Call of Nature	Quick decisions, but lasting effects
Second Look	Don't take things for granted
Tiphaine	One of life's wonderful people who make you smile
Grave Decision	An opportunity lost
Cocky Too's	Pub inhabitants blocking the bar and spouting off
Chariot Wheels	Frustrations of shopping
Hearsay	Broken relationships that time can distort

Altered Lives	Good, bad and ugly sides of Facebook
Tango for One	That you are responsible for yourself
The Easy Life	Recognition of disabled people's difficulties
Write or Wrong?	Warning on the death of our written word
Framed	Hypocrisy of presenting everything as perfect
Better or Worse	Judgemental people forgetting their own faults
Peoples Places	Don't miss out on seeing old friends
Brash Banned	On people who give criticism but cannot take it
Home Comforts	Count your blessings
Afterlife	The agony of bereavement
Stain of Shame	Condemnation of 9/11 terrorist attack
Deep Rooted	Enjoy winning, be stoic in adversity
Game to Lose	Ignore critical jealousy of "non-triers"
Last Dance Lesson	Enjoy people while they are with you
Last Request	Bravado of death until it looms
Locked Inside	Resist doubts and try to make yourself proud

Stolen	The numbing premature death of my sister
Voice Within	Confront your fears!
Final Destination	Walk life's road with as much dignity as possible
Loss of Life	Recognition that you cannot always prevail

Last Word...

If you have enjoyed these ramblings from the Psychy Poet, you can keep up to date with his dementia on Facebook, by searching for The Psychy Poet Laurie Wilkinson.

It would be truly appreciated if you could leave a review of this book on the website of your choice.